T0071117

Songs my Heart has Taught Me

Bob Chilcott

for SSA and piano

Vocal score

OXFORD
UNIVERSITY PRESS

OXFORD
UNIVERSITY PRESS

Great Clarendon Street, Oxford OX2 6DP,
United Kingdom

Oxford University Press is a department of the University of Oxford.
It furthers the University's objective of excellence in research, scholarship,
and education by publishing worldwide. Oxford is a registered trade mark of
Oxford University Press in the UK and in certain other countries

© Oxford University Press 2021 and 2022

Bob Chilcott has asserted his right under the Copyright, Designs
and Patents Act, 1988, to be identified as the Composer of this Work

Original version first published 2021. This version first published 2022.

Impression: 1

All rights reserved. No part of this publication may be reproduced,
stored in a retrieval system, or transmitted, in any form or by any means,
without the prior permission in writing of Oxford University Press

Permission to perform this work in public (except in the course of divine worship)
should normally be obtained from a local performing right licensing organization,
unless the owner or the occupier of the premises being used already holds
a licence from such an organization. Likewise, permission to make and
exploit a recording of these works should be obtained from a
local mechanical copyright licensing organization

Enquiries concerning reproduction outside the scope of the above
should be directed to the Music Rights Department, Oxford University Press,
at music.permissions.uk@oup.com or at the address above

ISBN 978–0–19–356290–5

Music and text origination by Katie Johnston
Printed in Great Britain on acid-free paper by
Halstan & Co. Ltd, Amersham, Bucks.

Contents

1. Unison 5
2. Harmony 11
3. Rhythm 18
4. Resolution 25

Composer's note

It was a privilege and an honour to be invited to write the Raymond Brock Memorial Commission for the ACDA National Conference in Dallas in 2021. I was asked to write something that embraced certain aspects of diversity: a rich, beautiful, and complex subject. I asked a brilliant young poet, Delphine Chalmers, to come on this journey with me to create this piece. As the National Conference ended up taking place virtually, this piece was first performed by the BBC Singers with pianist Anna Tilbrook, in a video recording to be broadcast to delegates. The piece was originally written for mixed voices, but some months later I re-worked it as this version for The Children's Chorus of Washington, D.C. and their Musical Director, Margaret Clark.

I have learnt so much from a life of extensive travel, through music and collaboration with many different people, but the overriding thing is that, as Maya Angelou says in her great poem 'Human Family', 'We are more alike, my friends, than we are unalike'. Throughout life, music has been my barometer; it has helped me to understand so many things and so many people, and I hold this deep in my heart, hence the title *Songs my Heart has Taught Me*. Delphine and I decided to use musical concepts as titles for the four songs that make up the work, exploring how these can help us to understand commonality.

The first song, 'Unison', is an anthem to unity that ends with the powerful line, 'The song of the future and the song of our souls are in unison'. 'Harmony', written in a more fluid, musical-theatre style, touches on people's need to be accepted, in a way like a note in a chord, in such a way that we can feel embraced, as Delphine writes so eloquently: 'In the song of shared acceptance lies an inner harmony.' The third song, 'Rhythm', is a spiky piece with a beat that tells of life's rhythm, of the pulse that the living all share, and it urges us to seize the day. Finally, in 'Resolution', the melody is spun by the singers over a simple, recurring chord structure. The poetic refrain is strongly influenced by the words of the 14th-century female mystic, Julian of Norwich: 'All shall be well, and all shall be well and all manner of thing shall be well.' The piece ends quietly and tonally, but of course does not completely resolve. That is the story of life.

Duration: *c.*11 minutes

Commissioned by the American Choral Directors Association as the 2021 Raymond W. Brock Memorial Commission.
This version is dedicated to Margaret Clark and the Children's Chorus of Washington, D.C.

Songs my Heart has Taught Me

Delphine Chalmers (b. 1998) **BOB CHILCOTT**

1. Unison

Music © Oxford University Press 2021 and 2022. Text © Delphine Chalmers. Used by permission.

Printed in Great Britain

OXFORD UNIVERSITY PRESS, MUSIC DEPARTMENT, GREAT CLARENDON STREET, OXFORD OX2 6DP
The Moral Rights of the Composer have been asserted. Photocopying this copyright material is ILLEGAL.

11
mp
hair, The whis - pers of the trees And the sto - ries we
mp
mp
16
p
write Are in u - ni - son, u - ni - son.
p
mm
p
When the
p
22
p
oo
oo
rip - ple of a smile Wea-thers dim - ples in - to stone And love breaks

27
mp
oo
on new shores, The surge of the tides And the
32
press of a hand Are in u - ni - son,
37
mf
f risoluto
u - ni - son. When the brav - est i - deals Take wing in soar - ing
u - ni - son. When the brav - est i - deals Take wing in soar - ing

42
flocks And make a home in warm - er skies, The
flocks And make a home in warm - er skies, The
47
pat - terns of the birds And the lives we weave Are in
pat - terns of the birds And the lives we weave Are in
52
mf
p
u - ni - son, u - ni - son.
mf
p
u - ni - son, u - ni - son.
mf
p

57
p
When dreams lin - ger in wak - ing thought Like teas - ing
p
mm
mm
62
con - stel - la - tions And hope fills e - ven hope - less hearts,
mm
67
mp
The song of the fu - ture And the song of our
mp
mp

71
p
souls Are in u - ni - son, u - ni - son.
p
mm u - ni - son.
p
76
a little slower
mp
The song of the fu - ture And the song of our souls Are in
p
mp
The song of the fu - ture And the song of our souls Are in
p
a little slower
mp
poco rit.
slower
82
pp
u - ni - son, u - ni - son, u - ni - son.
pp
u - ni - son, u - ni - son, u - ni - son.
poco rit.
slower
p
pp

2. Harmony

In the groove ♩ = c.100
SOPRANO 1
SOPRANO 2
ALTO
mf
Am I too co-mic?
In the groove ♩ = c.100
PIANO
mf
con Ped.
4
unis. mf
Or too me-lan-cho-lic? Too bold, or too old, or too vain? I
f
Too bold, or too old, or too vain? I
f
7
play the clown, brave their frowns. Is the
play the clown, brave their frowns. Is the

9
face in the mir - ror tru - ly mine?
face in the mir - ror, in the mir - ror tru - ly
11
mf
Am I too se - ri - ous?
mf
mine, tru - ly mine?
mf
14
3
3
Too loud, or too proud, or too
3
3
Or too mys - te - ri - ous? Too loud, or too proud, or too

16
f
free? I try on masks,
f
free? I try on masks,
f
18
act out parts. Is it real - ly so wrong to be me?
act out parts. Is it real - ly so wrong to be me?
21
ff
All these words vault like tum - blers.
ff
All these words vault like tum-blers, like tum - blers
ff

24
f
ah
ah
f
Stum - bling and strug - gling to land.
f
26
ff
f
I can soar through it all. May - be it's
ff
f
I can soar through it all. May - be it's
ff
f
28
time for my last cur - tain call, my last cur - tain
time for my last cur - tain call, my last cur - tain

30
mf
call.
mf
call, my last cur - tain call, cur - tain
mf
32
call.
34
mp più dolce
Trans -
mp più dolce
I've learned to play to a dif - f'rent crowd, Trans -
mp più dolce

36
mf
-pose in - to a ma - jor key. In the
-pose in - to a ma - jor key. In the
mf
mf
song of shared ac - cept - ance,
38
song of shared ac - cept - ance, of shared ac - cept - ance
song of shared ac - cept - ance, of shared ac - cept - ance
41
mp
har - mo - ny,
Lies an in - ner har - mo - ny,
mp
Lies an in - ner har - mo - ny,
mp

har - mo - ny,
44
mf
in - - ner har - mo - ny, in - - ner
in - - ner har - mo - ny, in - - ner
47
har - mo - ny,
mp
har - mo - ny, har - - mo - ny, lies an
har - mo - ny, har - - mo - ny, lies an
50
rit.
p
in - ner har - mo - ny, har - - mo - ny.
in - ner har - mo - ny, har - - mo - ny.
rit.
p

3. Rhythm

Strict tempo ♩ = c.92
TUTTI VOICES
PIANO
f
You can
hear it in the crac-kle of the break-ing dawn when the world is wak-ing up a-fresh. The
(tutti handclap)
blar-ing horns and your sti-fled yawn say to paint your co-lours on the day.

7
Clap it. Tap it. E - ven rap it. Feel the pulse and set life's beat.
9
unis.
S. 1
S. 2
Clap it. Tap it. E - ven rap it. Feel the pulse and set life's beat.
A.
Clap it. Tap it. E - ven rap it. Feel the pulse and set life's beat.
12
You can sense the
You can sense it in the swag-ger of a head-phoned guy when they

14
rhy- thm, sense the rhy- thm, sense the
pause to type a - no - ther text. The to and fro, and a - dre - na - line's flow de -
16
rhy- thm, rhy- thm, rhy- thm. Clap it. Tap it. E - ven rap it.
-clare love's time - less o - ver - ture. Clap it. Tap it. E - ven rap it.
18
Feel the pulse and set life's beat. Clap it. Tap it. E - ven rap it.
Feel the pulse and set life's beat. Clap it. Tap it. E - ven rap it.

20
Feel the pulse and set life's beat.
Feel the pulse and set life's beat.
22
You can note it in the beat-ing of your joy - ful heart when your
You can note the
24
steps e - cho on the street. The busk - er's riffs and his cheer - ful call fill the
rhy - thm, note the rhy - thm, note the

26
air with hum - ming me - lo - dies. Clap it. Tap it. E - ven rap it.
rhy - thm, rhy - thm, rhy - thm. Clap it. Tap it. E - ven rap it.
28
Feel the pulse and set life's beat. Clap it. Tap it. E - ven rap it.
Feel the pulse and set life's beat. Clap it. Tap it. E - ven rap it.
30
Feel the pulse and set life's beat. You can
Feel the pulse and set life's beat. You can

33
feel it in the sta - tic of the play - ful breeze when the world cries for you to dream. Your_
feel it in the sta - tic of the play - ful breeze when the world cries for you to dream. Your_
35
bud - ding thoughts and your soul's blank page say to seize each op - por - tu - ni - ty.
bud - ding thoughts and your soul's blank page say to seize each op - por - tu - ni - ty.
37
Clap it. Tap it. E - ven rap it. Feel the pulse and_ set life's beat.
Clap it. Tap it. E - ven rap it. Feel the pulse and_ set life's beat.

39
Clap it. Tap it. E - ven rap it. Feel the pulse, the pulse.
Clap it. Tap it. E - ven rap it. Feel the pulse, the pulse.
41
ff
Clap it. Tap it. E - ven rap it. Feel the pulse and set life's beat.
ff
Clap it. Tap it. E - ven rap it. Feel the pulse and set life's beat.
ff
43
Clap it. Tap it. E - ven rap it. Feel the pulse and set life's beat.
Clap it. Tap it. E - ven rap it. Feel the pulse and set life's beat.
fff

for Fern and Rob

4. Resolution

poco rit.
a tempo
12
unis.
S. 1
S. 2
stones thrown at my win - dow pane. For all the friends you miss, all the things you can - not fix, know
A.
stones thrown at my win - dow pane. For all the friends you miss, all the things you can - not fix, know
poco rit.
a tempo
15
mp
this: All will be safe, all will be sound, all will be bliss,
mp
this: All will be safe, all will be sound, all will be bliss,
mp
poco rit.
18
p
all will be safe, all will be sound, all will be bliss.
p
all will be safe, all will be sound, all will be bliss.
poco rit.
p

21
a tempo
mp
oo
oo
mp
Life has taught me a way to find the miss-ing chord I need, though mi-nor and ma-jor blend with-in my
a tempo
mp
24
oo
poco espress.
oo
me-mo-ry. The e-cho holds with-in it o-ther voi-ces. Love and
27
poco rit.
oo
oo
For all
loss en-twined in a sin-gle note like hearts and i-ni-tials carved in oak. For all
poco rit.

29
a tempo
words you can - not find and all that slips from sight and mind, know
words you can - not find and all that slips from sight and mind, know
a tempo
31
mf
this: All will be clear, all will be free, all will be bliss,
mf
this: All will be clear, all will be free, all will be bliss,
f
34
poco rit.
all will be clear, all will be free, all will be bliss.
all will be clear, all will be free, all will be bliss.
poco rit.
mf

a tempo
36
p dolce
Love has taught me a way to find the home key locked with - in. Though our
p dolce
Love has taught me a way to find the home key locked with - in. Though our
a tempo
p dolce
39
me - lo - dies wind and weave down ma - ny paths. Our mu - sic holds with - in a re - so -
me - lo - dies wind and weave down ma - ny paths. Our mu - sic holds with - in a re - so -
42
mp
-lu - tion.
oo
mp
-lu - tion.
Voi - ces sing - ing out a soft re - prieve like a
mp

44
poco rit.
p
a tempo
oo
For all mu - sic left to soar, and all
pro - mise car - ried on the breeze.
For all mu - sic left to soar, and all
poco rit.
a tempo
p
46
our un - writ - ten scores, know this:
mp
All will be safe, all will be calm,
our un - writ - ten scores, know this:
mp
All will be safe, all will be calm,
mp
49
mf
all will be bliss.
For all mu - sic left to soar and all
all will be bliss.
For all mu - sic left to soar and all
mf
mf

51
our un - writ - ten scores, know this:
our un - writ - ten scores, know this:
poco rit.
53
f
All will be safe, all will be calm, all will be bliss,
f
All will be safe, all will be calm, all will be bliss,
poco rit.
f
a little slower
rit.
55
mp
p
all will be safe, all will be calm, all will be bliss.
mp
p
all will be safe, all will be calm, all will be bliss.
a little slower
rit.
mp
p